The United States Presidents

MILLARD FILLMORE

ABDO Publishing Company

Heidi M.D. Elston

visit us at
www.abdopublishing.com

Published by ABDO Publishing Company, 8000 West 78th Street, Edina, Minnesota 55439.
Copyright © 2009 by Abdo Consulting Group, Inc. International copyrights reserved in all
countries. No part of this book may be reproduced in any form without written permission from the
publisher. The Checkerboard Library™ is a trademark and logo of ABDO Publishing Company.

Printed in the United States.

Cover Photo: Alamy
Interior Photos: Alamy pp. 10, 11, 14, 16, 19, 27, 29; American Political History pp. 5, 14, 17, 25;
     Corbis p. 12; Getty Images pp. 9, 13, 24; iStockphoto p. 32; Library of Congress pp. 15, 18;
     North Wind p. 21; Picture History pp. 10, 20, 23, 28

Editor: Megan M. Gunderson
Art Direction & Cover Design: Neil Klinepier
Interior Design: Jaime Martens

Library of Congress Cataloging-in-Publication Data

Elston, Heidi M. D., 1979-
  Millard Fillmore / Heidi M.D. Elston.
     p. cm. -- (The United States presidents)
  Includes bibliographical references and index.
  ISBN 978-1-60453-450-4
  1. Fillmore, Millard, 1800-1874--Juvenile literature. 2. Presidents--United States--Biography--
Juvenile literature. I. Title.
  E427.E45 2009
  973.6'4092--dc22
  [B]
                         2008035314

CONTENTS

MILLARD FILLMORE

Millard Fillmore was the thirteenth president of the United States. He led the country during one of the worst times in American history. The North and the South argued about slavery. Later, these arguments led to the American **Civil War**.

In 1828, Fillmore began working in politics. He was elected to the New York state legislature. Four years later, he won election to the U.S. House of Representatives.

In 1848, Zachary Taylor was elected president. Fillmore served as his vice president. Just 16 months after taking office, President Taylor died. Fillmore then became president.

As president, Fillmore helped pass the Compromise of 1850. He thought the compromise would solve the country's slavery problems. But neither the North nor the South was satisfied with the new laws. President Fillmore was so unpopular that he did not run for reelection.

Fillmore did what he thought was right for the country. He loved the United States and wanted to avoid war. He actively served his community and country throughout his life.

Timeline

1800 - On January 7, Millard Fillmore was born in Cayuga County, New York.

1823 - Fillmore began practicing law in East Aurora, New York.

1826 - On February 5, Fillmore married Abigail Powers.

1832 - Fillmore won election to the U.S. House of Representatives.

1834 - Fillmore joined the Whig Party.

1844 - Fillmore ran for governor of New York but lost a close election.

1847 - Fillmore was elected the comptroller of New York State.

1849 - On March 5, Fillmore became vice president under Zachary Taylor.

1850 - President Taylor died on July 9; on July 10, Fillmore became the thirteenth U.S. president; Congress passed the Compromise of 1850.

1853 - On March 4, Fillmore left the White House; Abigail Fillmore died.

1854 - The Treaty of Kanagawa opened Japanese ports to U.S. ships.

1856 - Once again, Fillmore ran for president. He lost the election to James Buchanan.

1858 - Fillmore married Caroline Carmichael McIntosh.

1867 - Fillmore started the Buffalo Club.

1874 - On March 8, Millard Fillmore died.

DID YOU KNOW?

Millard Fillmore was the first president to have a stepmother.

In 1855, Oxford University in Oxford, England, offered Fillmore an honorary degree. He refused it. The degree was written in Latin, which Fillmore couldn't read.

In 1819, Fillmore bought the first book he had ever owned. It was a dictionary.

Abigail Fillmore was the first First Lady to hold a job after getting married.

Abigail Fillmore started the White House library.

YOUNG MILLARD

Millard Fillmore was born in a log cabin in Cayuga County, New York, on January 7, 1800. He was the second child born to Nathaniel and Phoebe Fillmore. Millard had three sisters and five brothers.

As a boy, Millard worked on the family farm. Because he worked so much, he went to school only three months each year. Still he learned reading, writing, arithmetic, and geography.

When Millard was 14, he became an **apprentice** wool worker. He agreed to work for seven years. However after five years, Millard left the job. He paid his employer $30 to free him from the agreement.

At 19, Millard moved to Buffalo, New York. He found a job in a law office. Millard had not spent much time in school. But he was smart and loved to read. He got another part-time job teaching school.

FAST FACTS

BORN - January 7, 1800
WIVES - Abigail Powers (1798–1853), Caroline Carmichael McIntosh (1813–1881)
CHILDREN - 2
POLITICAL PARTY - Whig
AGE AT INAUGURATION - 50
YEARS SERVED - 1850–1853
VICE PRESIDENT - None
DIED - March 8, 1874, age 74

8

Millard's boyhood home

Millard studied law under a local judge. In 1823, he became a lawyer. For seven years, Millard practiced law in East Aurora, New York. Then, he moved his law firm to Buffalo. There, his business grew. Millard's law practice soon became one of the best known in the state!

FAMILY MAN AND CONGRESSMAN

On February 5, 1826, Fillmore married Abigail Powers. Abigail had been born in Stillwater, New York, in 1798. She was well educated and loved to read. From the time she was 16 years old, Abigail had taught school.

To bring in extra money, Abigail continued teaching until 1828. The Fillmores then raised two children. Millard Powers was born later that year. Mary Abigail followed in 1832.

Abigail Fillmore

Also in 1828, Fillmore began working in politics. That year, he was elected to the New York state legislature. At that time, people who couldn't pay their **debts** were commonly put in prison. Fillmore worked to pass laws forbidding this punishment for debt. Citizens of New York were happy with him.

Mary Abigail Fillmore

10

The Fillmores lived in this East Aurora home from 1826 to 1830.

In 1832, Fillmore won election to the U.S. House of Representatives. He served in Congress from 1833 to 1835 and from 1837 to 1843. In 1834, Fillmore joined the **Whig** Party.

Fillmore became a representative while Andrew Jackson was president. He supported the Whig Party's strong opposition to the president.

Fillmore served as chairman of the House Ways and Means Committee. As chairman, he helped make laws that taxed goods from other countries. These high taxes increased demand for American-made goods. This helped U.S. businesses, and the U.S. **economy** improved. As a result, Fillmore and the **Whig** Party grew popular.

As a congressman, Fillmore supported new inventions and businesses. He helped provide inventor Samuel F.B. Morse with $30,000 to help develop the **telegraph**. This invention helped Americans communicate over long distances.

Samuel Morse sent the first message over his telegraph in May 1844. It read, "What hath God wrought?"

NEW NOMINATIONS

Fillmore ran for governor of New York in 1844. He lost a close election. Fillmore then returned to his law practice. But, he did not give up on politics. In 1847, Fillmore was elected the state comptroller. In this position, he handled New York's money.

In 1848, the **Whig** Party chose Zachary Taylor to run for president. Fillmore was named his **running mate**. The **Democrats** nominated Senator Lewis Cass for

Lewis Cass

Taylor and Fillmore campaign poster

president. William Butler was chosen as Cass's **running mate**.

During the campaign, slavery was a vital issue. Taylor was a Southerner who owned slaves. Fillmore was an antislavery Northerner. Together, they appealed to many Americans.

Cass believed that the people in a territory should decide whether slavery should be allowed there. Because of Cass's views, his nomination angered

Martin Van Buren

many **Democrats**. Those members then split from the party. They voted for **Free-Soil** candidate Martin Van Buren. The split helped Taylor and Fillmore win the election by 36 electoral votes!

VICE PRESIDENT FILLMORE

Fillmore and Taylor did not meet until after the 1848 election. The two men came from very different backgrounds. They found they did not agree on many issues.

On March 5, 1849, Fillmore began his duties as vice president. His main duty was to govern the U.S. Senate.

As vice president, Fillmore felt shut out of President Taylor's administration.

At that time, many senators were caught up in bitter quarrels. They argued over issues such as slavery. Fillmore insisted that the senators respect each other. He brought order to the Senate.

In 1850, the Senate began **debating** a set of resolutions. Kentucky senator Henry Clay proposed them. He hoped they would end the slavery arguments. The resolutions became known as the Compromise of 1850.

President Taylor

President Taylor was against the compromise. So he would not pass it. Then everything changed. Zachary Taylor died on July 9, 1850. By law, Vice President Fillmore became president.

COMPROMISE OF 1850

Fillmore took the oath of office on July 10. He got right to work. President Fillmore supported the Compromise of 1850. So, he replaced Taylor's **cabinet** with men who also supported the compromise.

The compromise said that California should be admitted as a free state. It banned slave trading in Washington, D.C. And, it said the New Mexico and Utah territories could allow slavery if they wanted to.

The compromise included the Fugitive Slave Act. This act stated that runaway slaves could be captured and returned to their masters. Anyone who hid runaway slaves would be punished. The Fugitive Slave Act angered those against slavery.

Fugitive Slave Bill.

SUPREME COURT APPOINTMENT

BENJAMIN R. CURTIS - 1851

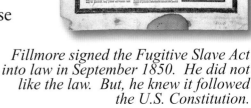

Fillmore signed the Fugitive Slave Act into law in September 1850. He did not like the law. But, he knew it followed the U.S. Constitution.

President Fillmore believed that without these new laws, a **civil war** would start. Then, the United States would break apart. Fillmore wanted to settle the slavery problem while preserving unity. In September, Congress passed the Compromise of 1850. President Fillmore was sure the slavery problem was solved.

Many people hoped Henry Clay's Compromise of 1850 would be the final solution to the slavery issue. Instead, it just delayed civil war for ten years.

THE THIRTEENTH PRESIDENT

President Fillmore also worked for trading rights with other countries. He sent Commodore Matthew Perry on an expedition to Japan. This led to the Treaty of Kanagawa in 1854. This treaty opened Japanese ports to U.S. ships. The United States profited from Japan. President Fillmore also lowered the U.S. postal rate from five to three cents.

While president, Fillmore spent most of his time dealing with the slavery issue. The Compromise of 1850 was not working. Americans still fought over slavery.

The Fugitive Slave Act was the biggest problem. President Fillmore found it difficult to enforce the act. Often, antislavery Northerners felt the president was siding with pro-slavery Southerners.

The Treaty of Kanagawa was the first treaty between Japan and any western country.

*Commodore
Matthew Perry*

Several incidents tested President Fillmore's ability to enforce the Fugitive Slave Act. One incident occurred in 1851. Maryland slave owner Edward Gorsuch traveled to Pennsylvania, a free state. Four of his slaves had escaped to Christiana, Pennsylvania. On September 11, a gunfight broke out. The slaves and local citizens fought Gorsuch, who died.

Afterward, 36 black men and 5 white men were charged with treason. Northerners were angry. They felt the slaves were only defending themselves.

Thus began the largest treason trial in U.S. history. The defendants were declared innocent. This ruling angered many Southerners. President Fillmore was caught between the North and the South. Neither side was happy with him.

Also that year, 2,000 people broke into a Syracuse, New York, jail. They freed a runaway slave. President Fillmore's attempts to punish anyone failed. The president's popularity continued to fall.

Fillmore believed the Compromise of 1850 would keep the United States together. Instead, it was pulling the country apart. By 1861, 11 states would leave the United States and form their own country.

PRESIDENT FILLMORE'S CABINET

JULY 10, 1850– MARCH 4, 1853

- **STATE** – Daniel Webster
  Edward Everett (from November 6, 1852)
- **TREASURY** – Thomas Corwin
- **WAR** – George Washington Crawford
  Charles Magill Conrad (from August 15, 1850)
- **NAVY** – William Alexander Graham
  John P. Kennedy (from July 26, 1852)
- **ATTORNEY GENERAL** – Reverdy Johnson
  John J. Crittenden (from August 14, 1850)
- **INTERIOR** – Thomas Ewing
  T.M.T. McKennan (from August 15, 1850)
  Alexander H.H. Stuart (from September 16, 1850)

AFTER THE WHITE HOUSE

The **Whig** Party did not nominate Fillmore to run for president in 1852. Fillmore knew he would not be chosen. Signing the Compromise of 1850 had angered antislavery Whigs.

Instead, the Whigs chose General Winfield Scott to run for president. Scott was against slavery. The Whigs hoped Scott would unite the party and win the election.

General Winfield Scott

Franklin Pierce served as president from 1853 to 1857.

But, the **Whigs** lost the election to **Democrat** Franklin Pierce. As a political party, the Whigs were almost finished. Fillmore was the last Whig president in U.S. history.

On March 4, 1853, Fillmore left the White House. He returned to Buffalo and his law practice. Just 26 days later, Abigail Fillmore died of **pneumonia**.

Fillmore was greatly saddened by the death of his wife. Just one year later, tragedy struck again. His daughter, Mary, died suddenly. Fillmore was heartbroken. To keep busy, he returned to politics.

KNOW-NOTHINGS

The United States and its politics were changing. Between the mid-1840s and the mid-1850s, nearly 3 million people **immigrated** to the United States. Germans moved to the Midwest, and Irish arrived in the East. Many native-born Americans felt threatened by this wave of immigrants.

In response, a secret group formed in the 1840s. Its members wanted to pass laws against these newcomers. The people in this group called themselves the Know-Nothings. Soon, the Know-Nothings organized a new political party. They called it the American Party.

The American Party wanted limitations placed on immigration and immigrants. Its members felt that immigrants should be barred from voting or holding public office. And, they wanted to impose a requirement on citizenship. Anyone seeking citizenship would first need to live in the country for 21 years.

The American Party gained power during the 1850s. It won many seats in Congress. But the party's popularity did not last long. It fell apart after 1856.

Fillmore did not agree with the American Party's anti-immigrant message.

RETURN TO BUFFALO

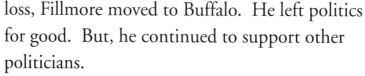

Fillmore decided to run for president again in 1856. The **Whig** Party and the American Party joined together. They made Fillmore their presidential candidate. John C. Frémont was the **Republican** Party candidate. The **Democrats** nominated James Buchanan.

In November, Fillmore lost the election to Buchanan. After this loss, Fillmore moved to Buffalo. He left politics for good. But, he continued to support other politicians.

In 1858, Fillmore married Caroline Carmichael McIntosh. The couple had many friends they enjoyed spending time with.

In Buffalo, Fillmore did much for his city. He supported the city's libraries. Fillmore also represented the Buffalo Board of Trade. He became the first **chancellor** of the University of Buffalo. And, he helped start the Buffalo General Hospital.

Caroline Fillmore

Fillmore founded and served as the first president of the Buffalo Historical Society. In 1867, he helped start a social club called the Buffalo Club. As the club's first president, Fillmore greeted many important visitors to the city.

Fillmore spent his last years close to his wife, who was ill. On March 8, 1874, Millard Fillmore died after suffering two **strokes**.

While Fillmore was president, slavery had divided the nation. He tried his best to solve this problem with wisdom and laws. Millard Fillmore was a modest man who worked hard to preserve the United States.

Outside Buffalo's city hall stands a statue in Fillmore's honor.

OFFICE OF THE PRESIDENT

BRANCHES OF GOVERNMENT

The U.S. government is divided into three branches. They are the executive, legislative, and judicial branches. This division is called a separation of powers. Each branch has some power over the others. This is called a system of checks and balances.

EXECUTIVE BRANCH

The executive branch enforces laws. It is made up of the president, the vice president, and the president's cabinet. The president represents the United States around the world. He or she oversees relations with other countries and signs treaties. The president signs bills into law and appoints officials and federal judges. He or she also leads the military and manages government workers.

LEGISLATIVE BRANCH

The legislative branch makes laws, maintains the military, and regulates trade. It also has the power to declare war. This branch consists of the Senate and the House of Representatives. Together, these two houses make up Congress. Each state has two senators. A state's population determines the number of representatives it has.

JUDICIAL BRANCH

The judicial branch interprets laws. It consists of district courts, courts of appeals, and the Supreme Court. District courts try cases. If a person disagrees with a trial's outcome, he or she may appeal. If the courts of appeals support the ruling, a person may appeal to the Supreme Court. The Supreme Court also makes sure that laws follow the U.S. Constitution.

QUALIFICATIONS FOR OFFICE

To be president, a person must meet three requirements. A candidate must be at least 35 years old and a natural-born U.S. citizen. He or she must also have lived in the United States for at least 14 years.

ELECTORAL COLLEGE

The U.S. presidential election is an indirect election. Voters from each state choose electors to represent them in the Electoral College. The number of electors from each state is based on population. Each elector has one electoral vote. Electors are pledged to cast their vote for the candidate who receives the highest number of popular votes in their state. A candidate must receive the majority of Electoral College votes to win.

TERM OF OFFICE

Each president may be elected to two four-year terms. Sometimes, a president may only be elected once. This happens if he or she served more than two years of the previous president's term.

The presidential election is held on the Tuesday after the first Monday in November. The president is sworn in on January 20 of the following year. At that time, he or she takes the oath of office:

I do solemnly swear (or affirm) that I will faithfully execute the office of President of the United States, and will to the best of my ability, preserve, protect and defend the Constitution of the United States.

LINE OF SUCCESSION

The Presidential Succession Act of 1947 defines who becomes president if the president cannot serve. The vice president is first in the line of succession. Next are the Speaker of the House and the President Pro Tempore of the Senate. If none of these individuals is able to serve, the office falls to the president's cabinet members. They would take office in the order in which each department was created:

Secretary of State

Secretary of the Treasury

Secretary of Defense

Attorney General

Secretary of the Interior

Secretary of Agriculture

Secretary of Commerce

Secretary of Labor

Secretary of Health and Human Services

Secretary of Housing and Urban Development

Secretary of Transportation

Secretary of Energy

Secretary of Education

Secretary of Veterans Affairs

Secretary of Homeland Security

BENEFITS

- While in office, the president receives a salary of $400,000 each year. He or she lives in the White House and has 24-hour Secret Service protection.

- The president may travel on a Boeing 747 jet called Air Force One. The airplane can accommodate 70 passengers. It has kitchens, a dining room, sleeping areas, and a conference room. It also has fully equipped offices with the latest communications systems. Air Force One can fly halfway around the world before needing to refuel. It can even refuel in flight!

- If the president wishes to travel by car, he or she uses Cadillac One. Cadillac One is a Cadillac Deville. It has been modified with heavy armor and communications systems. The president takes Cadillac One along when visiting other countries if secure transportation will be needed.

- The president also travels on a helicopter called Marine One. Like the presidential car, Marine One accompanies the president when traveling abroad if necessary.

- Sometimes, the president needs to get away and relax with family and friends. Camp David is the official presidential retreat. It is located in the cool, wooded mountains in Maryland. The U.S. Navy maintains the retreat, and the U.S. Marine Corps keeps it secure. The camp offers swimming, tennis, golf, and hiking.

- When the president leaves office, he or she receives Secret Service protection for ten more years. He or she also receives a yearly pension of $191,300 and funding for office space, supplies, and staff.

PRESIDENTS AND THEIR TERMS

PRESIDENT	PARTY	TOOK OFFICE	LEFT OFFICE	TERMS SERVED	VICE PRESIDENT
George Washington	None	April 30, 1789	March 4, 1797	Two	John Adams
John Adams	Federalist	March 4, 1797	March 4, 1801	One	Thomas Jefferson
Thomas Jefferson	Democratic-Republican	March 4, 1801	March 4, 1809	Two	Aaron Burr, George Clinton
James Madison	Democratic-Republican	March 4, 1809	March 4, 1817	Two	George Clinton, Elbridge Gerry
James Monroe	Democratic-Republican	March 4, 1817	March 4, 1825	Two	Daniel D. Tompkins
John Quincy Adams	Democratic-Republican	March 4, 1825	March 4, 1829	One	John C. Calhoun
Andrew Jackson	Democrat	March 4, 1829	March 4, 1837	Two	John C. Calhoun, Martin Van Buren
Martin Van Buren	Democrat	March 4, 1837	March 4, 1841	One	Richard M. Johnson
William H. Harrison	Whig	March 4, 1841	April 4, 1841	Died During First Term	John Tyler
John Tyler	Whig	April 6, 1841	March 4, 1845	Completed Harrison's Term	Office Vacant
James K. Polk	Democrat	March 4, 1845	March 4, 1849	One	George M. Dallas
Zachary Taylor	Whig	March 5, 1849	July 9, 1850	Died During First Term	Millard Fillmore

PRESIDENT	PARTY	TOOK OFFICE	LEFT OFFICE	TERMS SERVED	VICE PRESIDENT
Millard Fillmore	Whig	July 10, 1850	March 4, 1853	Completed Taylor's Term	Office Vacant
Franklin Pierce	Democrat	March 4, 1853	March 4, 1857	One	William R.D. King
James Buchanan	Democrat	March 4, 1857	March 4, 1861	One	John C. Breckinridge
Abraham Lincoln	Republican	March 4, 1861	April 15, 1865	Served One Term, Died During Second Term	Hannibal Hamlin, Andrew Johnson
Andrew Johnson	Democrat	April 15, 1865	March 4, 1869	Completed Lincoln's Second Term	Office Vacant
Ulysses S. Grant	Republican	March 4, 1869	March 4, 1877	Two	Schuyler Colfax, Henry Wilson
Rutherford B. Hayes	Republican	March 3, 1877	March 4, 1881	One	William A. Wheeler
James A. Garfield	Republican	March 4, 1881	September 19, 1881	Died During First Term	Chester Arthur
Chester Arthur	Republican	September 20, 1881	March 4, 1885	Completed Garfield's Term	Office Vacant
Grover Cleveland	Democrat	March 4, 1885	March 4, 1889	One	Thomas A. Hendricks
Benjamin Harrison	Republican	March 4, 1889	March 4, 1893	One	Levi P. Morton
Grover Cleveland	Democrat	March 4, 1893	March 4, 1897	One	Adlai E. Stevenson
William McKinley	Republican	March 4, 1897	September 14, 1901	Served One Term, Died During Second Term	Garret A. Hobart, Theodore Roosevelt

PRESIDENT	PARTY	TOOK OFFICE	LEFT OFFICE	TERMS SERVED	VICE PRESIDENT
Theodore Roosevelt	Republican	September 14, 1901	March 4, 1909	Completed McKinley's Second Term, Served One Term	Office Vacant, Charles Fairbanks
William Taft	Republican	March 4, 1909	March 4, 1913	One	James S. Sherman
Woodrow Wilson	Democrat	March 4, 1913	March 4, 1921	Two	Thomas R. Marshall
Warren G. Harding	Republican	March 4, 1921	August 2, 1923	Died During First Term	Calvin Coolidge
Calvin Coolidge	Republican	August 3, 1923	March 4, 1929	Completed Harding's Term, Served One Term	Office Vacant, Charles Dawes
Herbert Hoover	Republican	March 4, 1929	March 4, 1933	One	Charles Curtis
Franklin D. Roosevelt	Democrat	March 4, 1933	April 12, 1945	Served Three Terms, Died During Fourth Term	John Nance Garner, Henry A. Wallace, Harry S. Truman
Harry S. Truman	Democrat	April 12, 1945	January 20, 1953	Completed Roosevelt's Fourth Term, Served One Term	Office Vacant, Alben Barkley
Dwight D. Eisenhower	Republican	January 20, 1953	January 20, 1961	Two	Richard Nixon
John F. Kennedy	Democrat	January 20, 1961	November 22, 1963	Died During First Term	Lyndon B. Johnson
Lyndon B. Johnson	Democrat	November 22, 1963	January 20, 1969	Completed Kennedy's Term, Served One Term	Office Vacant, Hubert H. Humphrey
Richard Nixon	Republican	January 20, 1969	August 9, 1974	Completed First Term, Resigned During Second Term	Spiro T. Agnew, Gerald Ford

PRESIDENT	PARTY	TOOK OFFICE	LEFT OFFICE	TERMS SERVED	VICE PRESIDENT
Gerald Ford	Republican	August 9, 1974	January 20, 1977	Completed Nixon's Second Term	Nelson A. Rockefeller
Jimmy Carter	Democrat	January 20, 1977	January 20, 1981	One	Walter Mondale
Ronald Reagan	Republican	January 20, 1981	January 20, 1989	Two	George H.W. Bush
George H.W. Bush	Republican	January 20, 1989	January 20, 1993	One	Dan Quayle
Bill Clinton	Democrat	January 20, 1993	January 20, 2001	Two	Al Gore
George W. Bush	Republican	January 20, 2001	January 20, 2009	Two	Dick Cheney
Barack Obama	Democrat	January 20, 2009			Joe Biden

"An honorable defeat is better than a dishonorable victory."
Millard Fillmore

WRITE TO THE PRESIDENT

You may write to the president at:

**The White House
1600 Pennsylvania Avenue NW
Washington, DC 20500**

You may e-mail the president at:

comments@whitehouse.gov

GLOSSARY

apprentice - a person who learns a trade or a craft from a skilled worker.

cabinet - a group of advisers chosen by the president to lead government departments.

chancellor - a university president.

civil war - a war between groups in the same country. The United States of America and the Confederate States of America fought a civil war from 1861 to 1865.

debate - a contest in which two sides argue for or against something.

debt - something owed to someone, usually money.

Democrat - a member of the Democratic political party. When Millard Fillmore was president, Democrats supported farmers and landowners.

economy - the way a nation uses its money, goods, and natural resources.

Free-Soil - a political party that had power between 1848 and 1854. Its members opposed the extension of slavery into U.S. territories and the admission of slave states into the Union.

immigration - entry into another country to live. A person who immigrates is called an immigrant.

pneumonia (nu-MOH-nyuh) - a disease that affects the lungs and may cause fever, coughing, or difficulty breathing.

Republican - a member of the Republican political party. When Millard Fillmore was president, Republicans supported business and strong government.

running mate - a candidate running for a lower-rank position on an election ticket, especially the candidate for vice president.

stroke - a sudden loss of consciousness, sensation, and voluntary motion. This attack of paralysis is caused by a rupture to a blood vessel of the brain, often caused by a blood clot.

telegraph - a device that uses electricity to send coded messages over wires.

Whig - a member of the Whig political party that was very strong in the early 1800s but ended in the 1850s. Whigs supported laws that helped business.

WEB SITES

To learn more about Millard Fillmore, visit ABDO Publishing Company on the World Wide Web at **www.abdopublishing.com**. Web sites about Millard Fillmore are featured on our Book Links page. These links are routinely monitored and updated to provide the most current information available.

INDEX